NONPROFIT

REALITIES

Everybody Must Face

A 1-Hour Crash Circuit
Through Facts and
Figures.

with
Dr. Amanda N. Gibson

NONPROFIT REALITIES

Everybody Must Face

A 1-Hour Crash Circuit Through Facts and Figures.

Dr. Amanda N. Gibson

This book is dedicated to Enrique M. Triay, for it was his suggestion which made it be ☺

Dr. Amanda N. Gibson is one of the few people who can communicate profound ideas to audiences of all types–from CEOs to career transitioners to those new to the field.

She is an Assistant Professor with the Broward College and earned her interdisciplinary Ph.D. in 2013 from the University of Phoenix with a concentration in Business Administration. She is also the founder of ANG Management Coaching and Consulting (ANG-MCC), a woman-owned provider of training, leadership development, and consulting services to community-based organizations.

Dr. Amanda N. Gibson has over 15 years of multi-faceted work experience, with notable achievements in teaching, mentoring, project management, financial environment, and consulting. Her comprehensive background and exposure to cultural diversity gained by working abroad and in non-profit organizations complement the scholarly degrees. Passionate about Nonprofit Management, Entrepreneurship and Leadership, Dr. Gibson is a keen researcher and scholar while equally interested to share her accumulated experience through consulting, teaching and writing.

Table of Contents

Social entrepreneurs and their networks demonstrate an unrelenting focus on systemic social change that disregards institutional an organizational norms and boundaries; they are disruptive change-agents.

(Nicholls, 2006)

Intro

Numerous case studies and scholarly articles bring forth the necessity of integrating behavior and strategy in shaping organizations. It used to be that these activities were analyzed, studied, and implemented separately. The result of such a tactic was – is – an organization lacking in flexibility and oftentimes displaying difficulties in implementing its mission statement.

As nowadays business world is in continued transformation, the only winning tactic is flexibility, with almost real-time feedback from measures implemented. This way the organization benefits from a strategy clearly oriented towards future results, resources more efficiently allocated towards executing strategic initiatives and outcomes that assess performance. While strategy matches external opportunities with internal strengths, behavioral studies identify and strengthen the very core of a company: "the most resilient building blocks available to organizations as they respond to external demands are the sets of semiautonomous groups, capable of self-regulation ... together with the larger networks of groups organized into functionally interdependent primary work systems" (Scott, 2003).

Some Background Information:

Let's discuss a non-profit corporation with a numbers of subsidiaries, all recognized as nonprofit organizations. This Corporation receives the majority of revenue from state governments, as contract funding for programs. One of its subsidiaries, Family Rehabilitation Services, receives the majority of its revenues from the Medicaid program as reimbursement, under a prospective, case-mix based, rate of payment system for the care and services rendered. The Corporation is centralized at administrative level (Payroll, HR, Accounts Payable and Receivable, IT) while in same time having separate budgets and leadership for each of the service-providing units affording them a considerable level of autonomy.

How Do We Measure a Nonprofit's Effectiveness?

Effectiveness in nonprofit organizations is a much discussed concept, lacking a definite and unanimously agreed upon definition – or measurable parameters. It is a matter of comparison, either to similar organizations or to the same organization at earlier times – and even to some ideal. It is also multidimensional, presenting multiple criteria which can often be independent of one another (Herman & Renz, 2008). In their analysis, Baruch & Ramalho (2006) found that majority of studies used preponderantly nonfinancial criteria: "employee satisfaction, customer orientation, quality and public image" (as cited by Herman & Renz, 2008). Its importance in stakeholders' view causes continuous efforts by nonprofits' managers to measure and improve management practices. For example, Provan & Milvard's (1995) studies found efficiency measured by outcomes: client and family assessments were closely correlated, while staff assessments were not. Therefore, nonprofit leaders have to closely interrelate with key stakeholders to establish what are the efficiency criteria and what changes may intervene (Herman & Renz, 2008).

From an economic point of view, characteristic to non-profit firms is a so-called self-sufficiency, meaning that people controlling them derive utility from fulfilling the organization's mission more than anything else. As Valentinov (2008) explains, "this characteristic demarcates managerial utility maximization in nonprofit firms from that in for-profit ones ...but these forms do not represent the official organizational goals. According to James and Rose-Ackerman (1986), "nonprofit managers maximize utility because they cannot maximize profit due to the non-distribution constraint" (as cited by Valentinov, 2008).

Due to the specifics of the analyzed company, work is performed in close proximity of other coworkers and supervisors, leading to nonverbal immediacy. Mehrabian (1967) defines it as "the communicative behaviors used to enhance closeness and reduce physical or psychological distance between individuals". Richmond and McCroskey (2000) consider that nonverbal immediacy between subordinates and supervisors "enhance perceptions of supervisor credibility, attraction and affect" and in consequence "increase subordinate motivation and job satisfaction" (as cited by Goodboy & McCroskey, 2008).

But we'll get back to these aspects in a short while - especially from an organizational and HR points of view.

~   0 ~

Nonprofit Realities

Does it Pay to Work for a Nonprofit?

Historically consistent, nonprofit wages have been lower than in for-profit organizations. This has been explained as either "labor donations", banking on employees' desire to contribute to the realization of the mission of their nonprofit firms (Preston, 1989) or as screening devices for selecting only those managers with non-pecuniary interest, "who can restrain their desire for earning profit" (Young, 1983). Yet, none of these reasons have been proved necessary – nor sufficient to make nonprofit firms "neither free from nor immune to opportunism" as Valentinov (2008) clearly states.

Differences in wages and compensations, from the lowest to the topmost level, compound the already difficult situation of leadership in nonprofits. As Tierney (2005) correctly assumes, "the greatest rewards of nonprofit careers will always be intangible, but that doesn't mean that compensation doesn't matter. Indeed, as nonprofit managers face increasingly complex challenges and are judged by much rigorous performance standards, their tougher, riskier jobs will require commensurate rewards". Otherwise the sector's leadership deficit will intensify in the next few years. As the sector is expanding, leaders' numbers are dwindling. With some present leaders retiring, burned-out or pursuing more attractive opportunities, most nonprofits find themselves too small to offer career development for tomorrow's leaders, and lacking resources for recruiting. According to a study of leadership requirements of US nonprofits with revenues greater than $250,000 carried out by Bridgespan, in 2006 were needed 56,000 new senior managers. Same study estimates that "over the decade from 2007 to 2016, they will need to attract and develop some 640,000 new senior leaders – or the equivalent of 2.4 <u>times</u> the number currently employed. To put this challenge in context, filling the gap would require recruiting more than 50 percent of every MBA graduating class, at every university across the country, every year for the next decade." (Tierney, 2005).

Any Solutions?

As alternative, executive coaching has "received increased attention over the past decade as a mechanism to build capacity and address issues of burnout and turnover among executives" (Fisher & Beimers, 2009). According to studies led by A.E.Casey Foundation (2004) and Bell, Moyers & Wolfred (2006), "turnover among nonprofit executives will continue to be substantial, with an estimated 65 percent of current executives nationally

planning a transition within five years".
Unfortunately, studies find nonprofits unprepared to
handle this transition, more than half of those
surveyed lacking an executive succession plan
(Fisher & Beimers, 2009).

Another identified direction of change would
be the use of Organization Development
practitioners, which can help nonprofits "adapt to
changing environments, identify priorities, and
strengthen leadership in ways that are consistent
with underlying values of social justice, individual
respect, and collaboration" (Seashore & Seashore,
2006). Directions of action would be building
leadership capacity, solving organization problems
systemically, aligning strategies, systems and
processes organization-wide, and effectively apply

organizational change principles (Wirtenberg et al, 2007).

What Theories are in Play on a Nonprofit Field?

Well, most of the organizational behavior theories reviewed in the Organizational Behavior Taxonomy are manifested in nonprofit organizations, in different degrees of incorporation.

☐ Goal-setting theory of motivation

Theory states that performance and job satisfaction are directly influences by motivation. People can set up goals, use information from their subconscious if it is relevant to said goals, and act towards what they want to accomplish.

As wages are lower in nonprofits therefore the interest in holding such a job is non-pecuniary, employees' performance is influenced by motivation. Their job satisfaction is brought by the quality of the services provided and in general by accomplishing their designed outcomes.

□ <u>Contingency theory of organizations</u>

To be successful, organizations must balance differentiation and integration. By setting units with different, but high level of expertise and insuring good integration amongst them companies have best odds of becoming highly adaptive to changes.

Therefore, a nonprofit is one of the best places to observe differentiation and integration. For example, in providing services to mentally retarded population, a company employs direct care staff, clinicians, nurses, doctors, supervisors, and administrative personnel – each of them with different skills but with the same goal – the wellbeing of their persons served.

☐ <u>Knowledge-based theory</u>

Theory posits that knowledge, amount and usage, are more important than physical and financial resources in providing a firm with competitive advantage. Such knowledge can consist of workers' expertise, product designs, customer databases or efficient processes.

Again, a nonprofit seems to be the best example for the theory, as financial resources are scarce and physical ones are much less needed than in regular organizations. Being a service provider, such an organization values most the expertise, skills and qualities of the workers.

☐ Corporate demography

Theory sustains that organizational diversity is an essential factor in corporate demography. By embracing a high diversity, organization is obtaining a greater economic success thru better knowledge of the characteristics of the targeted customers.

A byproduct of low wages, a nonprofit's employee pool is formed mostly by recent émigrés, from all geographic areas. As services are provided regardless of the clients' origin, oftentimes organizations require a specific skill among staff – speakers of Creole, or Mandarin for example.

☐ Cultural feminism

Theory mentions the "glass ceiling" encountered by women in their career after a certain level. Until now, women had to change their behavior hoping to have a better chance in competing in a patriarchal society.

According to the US government's Glass Ceiling Commission, "although women held 46 percent of jobs in the United States and more than half of the master's degrees being awarded, 95 percent of senior managers were men. This commission also found that female managers' earnings averaged 68 percent of their male counterparts'. In 2005, women accounted for 47 percent of the U.S. workforce and less than 8 percent of its top managers, averaging only 72 percent of their male colleagues' salaries "(Sampson & Moore, 2008)

☐ <u>Organizational diversity</u>

Theory considers diversity in what concerns mainly gender and race, as the majority of managers are still white males with women and minorities abiding by their norms and values.

In what concerns the workers and low to medium management, nonprofits can claim great organizational diversity – attributable again to low wages. At higher management levels it slowly falls towards the old patterns, with mostly whites males and only rarely a woman or minority person representing the odd exception.

Our best hope for the future of humanity lies in the power and effectiveness of socially motivated, highly empowered, individuals to fight for changes in the way we live, think, and behave.

Nonprofit Realities

What Are We Dealing With

So we're looking at a nonprofit Corporation with centralized, vertical hierarchy of command and a high degree of specialization and formalization. Work is divided into precise tasks and job descriptions clearly describe the skills, specific responsibilities, and procedures. Job design focuses mainly on the tasks to be performed. Coordination of departments is done at top-level management and upward communication consists mainly in reports, forecasts, and schedules.

Considering all aspects one can conclude that at present this organization is mechanistic-type, largely ignoring the human aspects and dynamics. Consequently, due to its difficulties of coping with rapid change, runs the risk of losing ground to competitors. Best strategy would be implementing changes prone to transform it into a post-modern, team-based organization, with coaching-like leaders.

OK, Then What Should I Do?

First step in such undertaking would be an in-depth analysis, focused on identifying the strong points of present situation and what will be preserved. Studies show that mechanistic structures are characterized by efficiency and a high degree of differentiation – which are desirable in any organization. Next step would be to implement an evolutionary change, trying to "improve, adapt, and adjust strategy and structure incrementally to accommodate to changes taking place in the environment" (Jones, 2007). During the past two decades, organizations underwent many types of transformations – "downsizing, delayering, reorganization (e.g. into small product divisions), total quality management, reengineering, self-managed teams, outsourcing, and partnering" (Yukl, 2006). A direction this paper will take is to examine establishing a team-based organization, comparing and contrasting its effectiveness and providing recommendations for development to meet the needs of modern organizations.

Researchers use different terms for team-based organizations, including "participative" (Yukl, 2006), "horizontal" (Jones, 2007), "networked"

(Clawson, 2006) or "infocracies" (Clawson, 2006). Most such organizations have also in common self-managing teams, executives as mentors and diversity.

In team-based organizations, teams have access to information, decision-making responsibility to a certain degree and access to resources for fulfilling projects and tasks. While teams might not always have a leader, "leadership is bound to remain important because even self-managing teams are seldom afforded full decision-making authority, and key decisions remain in the hands of those individuals explicitly designated as leaders" (Morgeson, 2005 as cited by Kearney & Gebert, 2009).

☐ <u>Mentorship</u>

Another important role for a leader in a team-based organization is as mentor, facilitator of team performance. Most leaders successful in such endeavor present some specific traits: extraversion, agreeableness, conscientiousness, emotional adjustment, and openness to experience (Judge & Bono, 2000). Researchers demonstrated significant relationships between personality and work-related outcomes, so it is up to such leaders to establish the work climate across the organization. Discussing about performance, Day & Bedeian (2009) state, "a positive work climate might compensate for low self-esteem such that there is little difference in work performance between high and low self-esteem workers in this type of environment. A difference between groups may be found in negative climates

39

(with high-esteem workers performing better), perhaps because high self-esteem compensates for a poor work climate". Finally yet importantly, leaders have to handle carefully the performance appraisals, which lately escalated so more and more people are getting highest rating but without the rewards being tied to evaluation sending thus mixed signals: "employees see no connection between what they do and what they're paid" (Clawson, 2006). Another valid aspect is the fact that unidirectional feedback is incomplete, should be taken in consideration also feedback from peers, customers and subordinates.

☐ Diversity

In what concerns diversity in teams, leaders can influence the information-decision-making perspective, as they "foster the elaboration and in-depth processing of the broader range of task-relevant information that is available in heterogeneous teams" (Kearney & Gebert, 2009). Diverse teams utilize a greater range of task-relevant resources, so organizations should consider ways of facilitating it, while preventing "dysfunctional social categorization" from diminishing the degree of collaboration and integration of perspectives. According to Trompenaars & Hampden-Turner (2002), leaders must "manage culture," because leaders who recognize and reconcile value differences are more successful. Finally, Manz & Sims (2001) introduce the SuperLeader, which "encourages initiative, self-responsibility, self-confidence, self-goal-setting, positive opportunity thinking, and self-problem-solving."

☐ <u>Leadership Style</u>

"We fail to grasp the essence of leadership that is relevant to the modern age and hence we cannot agree even on the standards by which to measure, recruit and reject it.... How do leaders lead followers without being wholly led by followers?" (Burns, 1978). How can leaders make the most of their followers? What is the best way to organize a team to go through a certain process and achieve the desired outcome? Shaping an organization starts with investing in leadership capacity, by choosing individuals with not only technical expertise but also coachable, flexible, and entrepreneurial. After all, learning – for individuals, teams or organizations – is the most important source of competitive advantage.

"Leaders who were rated by their subordinates as transformational were more satisfying and motivating to subordinates, were more likely to be associated with subordinates who expressed commitment to their organizations, and were more likely to be rated by the leader's supervisor as effective leaders"(Judge & Bono, 2000).

~ 0 ~

Nonprofit Realities

Amitai Etzioni (The Third Sector and Domestic Missions, 1973) suggested that neither the state (public sector) nor the market (private sector) alone could catalyze the necessary innovations and reforms of society but rather the source would be a "third alternative".

Nonprofit Realities

☐ <u>The Ethical Aspect</u>

Advocating the introduction of ethics programs, Kaptein (2009) is asserting that every component of such a program has the potential to shape the ethical culture of an organization. A firm's ethical conformity is usually the result of institutional environment and societal norms – but also of that firm's identity (Martin and Johnson, 2008). In their study, Harcourt, Lam and Harcourt (2005) find that organizations appear to be responsive to both traditional, economic pressures to maximize profits and minimize costs but also to institutional pressures to enhance legitimacy by not discriminating.

So our Corporation's policies and procedures stipulate equal treatment of the employees, regardless of their gender or ethnicity. Any allegation of misconduct is thoroughly investigated and even such instances are rare. The only conflicts arising are between personal customs, values – and company's ethical standards. Employees coming from backgrounds discriminating towards women, for example, may have difficulties complying with company's ethical standards. It is our opinion that both the organization and such employees could benefit from the implementation of a diversity program, providing training on equal opportunity.

☐ Corporate Demography

Back to organizational diversity, as it is an essential factor in corporate demography. By embracing a high diversity, organization is obtaining a greater economic success thru better knowledge of the characteristics of the targeted customers. A byproduct of low wages, a nonprofit's employee pool is formed mostly by recent émigrés, from all geographic areas. As services are provided regardless of the clients' origin, oftentimes organizations require a specific skill among staff – speakers of Creole, or Mandarin for example.

Considering diversity in what concerns mainly gender and race, the majority of managers are still white males with women and minorities abiding by their norms and values.

In what concerns the workers and low to medium management, nonprofits can claim great organizational diversity – attributable again to low wages. At higher management levels it slowly falls towards the old patterns, with mostly white males and only rarely a woman or minority person representing the odd exception.

Joseph A. Banks (1972) first coined the term 'social entrepreneur' in his seminal work on social reform (The Sociology of Social Movements), noting that managerial skills could be deployed to address social problems, as well as business challenges.

Nonprofit Realities

Cultural Pluralism - What is That?

In studies of international joint ventures and multinational teams, it has been shown that cultural differences can cause many difficulties. Zhang (2003) eloquently presents the dichotomies in various multicultural teams. For a Japanese firm operating in the US, the view of job responsibilities varied according to race: from expectations of well-defined (Americans) to a diffused understanding (Japanese). In addition, "the Americans saw clear link between authority, responsibility, and risk, whereas the link was much weaker for the Japanese who tended to think from a long-term perspective.

In effect, the subculture and the differentiation fall along national culture lines" (Kleinberg, 1989 as cited by Zhang, 2003). In the case of a French company in Slovenia, problematic was the authority in superior-subordinate settings. From the French's point of view, "authority derived from one's administrative position and hierarchical distance between the supervisor and the lower level employees. From the Slovenian point of view, however, there was a need for equality among all members and authority should be based on the supervisors' professional knowledge and practical skills" (Globokar, 1997 as cited by Zhang, 2003). In Thailand subsidiaries of American multinationals, the communication culture was the source of frustrations – the Thais "preferred politeness, whereas the Americans valued directness" (Stage, 1999 as cited by Zhang, 2003).

Gender and cultural differences

According to Baker (1998), South Korean conglomerates (or chaebols) "are owned and controlled by the founding family. Even top managers who actually run the company are often overshadowed and easily overruled by them. Sometimes this means questionable investment decisions. This atmosphere stifles potentially constructive dissent, frustrates talented younger workers, and makes others passive while they wait the 20 to 30 years to climb the hierarchy and get a bigger desk with decision making authority." The majority of the transactional leaders in South Korea base the workers promotions and job performance on the sole objective of reaching set goals within a set period.

Turner and Monk-Turner (2007) state "In 1988, 83.3 percent of all female workers were employed in three broad occupational categories. Few women (5.4 percent) worked as professional, technical, or administrative workers. By 1998, 11.5 percent of female workers were employed as professionals. The highest paid occupational categories, in South Korea, have the lowest percentage of female workers. Women benefit from additional educational experience, though less so than holds for men, and from being in a union (in 1988). Women are penalized, in terms of occupational status prestige, when working in large firms and when married." Statistics have proven this mirrors Japan's working population as well.

Yang-Im and Trim (2008) discusses cultural and gender differences by stating " In South Korea, men benefit occupationally more than women from additional educational experience and from working in large firms. Men are penalized by being in a union. Women, on the other hand, benefit occupationally from additional educational experience, though not as much as is true for men, and from being in a union. With regard to occupational status attainment, women are penalized by working in large firms and from being married." Regardless of the study, women in South Korea are not equal to men in terms of job classification, funds, or security.

~   O ~

Nonprofit Realities

Back to Our Example...

Remember our nonprofit Corporation. Just like it, at present still many organizations have a centralized, vertical hierarchy of command and a high degree of specialization and formalization – what Leininger (1997) calls ethnocentric approach. Work is divided into precise tasks and job descriptions clearly describe the skills, specific responsibilities, and procedures. Job design focuses mainly on the tasks to be performed. Coordination of departments in such organizations is done at top-level management and upward communication consists mainly in reports, forecasts, and schedules. Considering all aspects one can conclude that such an organization is mechanistic-type, largely ignoring the human aspects and dynamics. Therefore, due to its difficulties of coping with rapid change, might run the risk of losing ground to competitors. Best strategy in this case would be implementing changes prone to transform it into a post-modern, team-based organization, with coaching-like leaders.

So, Can We Make It Be Better?

Organizations built for flexibility, performance, and speed are "ruled by high-performing teams with real decision-making clout and accountability for results, rather than by committees that pass decisions up to the next level or toss them over the wall into the nearest silo"

(Guttman, 2008). Also, "the most resilient building blocks available to organizations as they respond to external demands are the sets of semiautonomous groups, capable of self-regulation ... together with the larger networks of groups organized into functionally interdependent primary work systems" (Scott, 2003).

Clawson (2006) agreed that leadership is becoming dispersed in organizations, and went a step further to explain *how* leaders help others become self-leaders and effective employees. He argued that leadership occurs at three levels of basic human interaction: visible behavior, conscious thought, and semi-conscious values, assumptions, beliefs, and expectations. Level three leadership applies in several areas of team-based. First, the model "seeks to understand the basic assumptions and values of employees and match them...with the goal and strategic direction of the firm" (Clawson, 2006). This objective clearly

matches one of the key roles of leaders in any organization, which is to communicate strategy and effectively connect with individual team members. Second, level three leadership is concerned with ever-changing team contexts and effectively managing these changes. Third, level three leadership promotes diversity in team-based work units and leaders who respect members regardless of race, gender, or religion. In any competitive organization, leaders should facilitate for teams to have access to information, decision-making responsibility to a certain degree and access to resources for fulfilling projects and tasks. While teams might not always have a leader, "leadership is bound to remain important because even self-managing teams are seldom afforded full decision-making authority, and key decisions remain in the hands of those individuals explicitly designated as leaders" (Morgeson, 2005 as cited by Kearney & Gebert, 2009).

~ *0* ~

Beware How You Communicate!

Communication is oftentimes done through marketing. Most successful marketing campaigns bank on known imagery and notions. In addition, the information thusly transmitted can stand in as foundation for knowledge, influencing thinking and understanding. The issue here is that oftentimes the representation used to reinforce a product or service's image can be demeaning to persons or groups of persons, being discriminatory or sexist – and the harm is compounded considering the future effects as the process shapes meaning. The use of demeaning, stereotypical clichés is especially misleading in the marketplace, where the visual and semiotic literacy is questionable. Oftentimes advertisements present women as product while masculinity is associated with success, skill and economic power.

More Ethics

Advocating the introduction of ethics programs, Kaptein (2009) is asserting that every component of such a program has the potential to shape the ethical culture of an organization. As example, he offers the relationship between ethical culture and the pre-employment screenings as well as the ethics hotlines, which are indicatives of an integrated ethics program. A firm's ethical conformity is usually the result of institutional environment and societal norms – but also of that firm's identity (Martin and Johnson, 2008). In what concerns laws, Cheney (2006) advises that "law is generally a moral minimum", and companies would be well advised to "try to act a bit above that line." This is especially important if the risk from a high harm product is not immediately apparent. Jones and Middleton (2006) warn that "companies knowing that consumers are unable to identify the added risk associated with their products may find themselves bearing increased liability if actual harm to the consumers results." For multinational corporations, Weismann (2008) observes that compliance plans are "a necessary cost of doing business...the plans merely serve to cushion the blow in the event of regulatory action".

In an environment where personal lifestyles are controlled very rigidly, laws are strongly enforced, and the justice system has no international or host country agreements, the only leadership. Some leaders could engage in unethical behavior because they trust they will not get caught, hope their relationship with their stakeholders will not be affected or do not believe their behavior is unethical. This is defined by Drumwright and Murphy (2004) as moral myopia: a distortion of moral vision ranging from shortsightedness to near blindness, which affects an individual's perception of an ethical dilemma. A leader's strong ethical policy has considerable benefits for employees, whose satisfaction with supervisors and coworkers is increased by ethics training, ethical values and positive business practices. In such situation, Valentine (2009) observes an increased positive work attitude, because "guidance should strengthen the ethical values and practices of work colleagues, thus enhancing their acceptability in the minds of colleagues and augmenting perceptions that the company is indeed ethical". The conclusion would be that organizations – particularly multinational ones, should be extremely aware of this issue – and avoid bad faith and damaging representation.

"For social entrepreneurs the social mission is explicit and central. This obviously affects how social entrepreneurs perceive and assess opportunities. Mission-related impact becomes the central criterion, not wealth creation."

(Dees, 1998)

Nonprofit Realities

A Brief Conclusion:

The actual environment for nonprofit organizations is extremely challenging: changing healthcare climate, increased competition for personnel, emphasis on the scientific evaluation of the programs. Even though it's widely recognized that "organizations that invest adequately in their infrastructures and long term planning are the ones that will survive" (Applegate, 2008) nonprofits are challenged more than ever due to the paucity of resources. This implies focus on immediate, urgent needs – leaving aside the examination of the organization, environment and future. Shortage of funds means also inability to hire external help and assistance for capacity building and organizational development, which hinders effectiveness, efficiency and growth.

The steps nonprofits should take are: develop systems, strategies and processes as necessary, solve organizational problems systemically, create a culture supporting collaboration and alliances. Avoid leadership crisis. Compensate for the lacks the infrastructure business world has, for executive search, job boards and outsourcing services.

And let's not forget the Social Entrepreneurship.

More about that in a future book!

... Social entrepreneurs are practical dreamers who have the talent and the skill and the vision to solve [social] problems; to change the world for the better . . . Social entrepreneurs have a vision of the future and will stop at nothing to see that future come true. It is up to [all of you] to help them succeed in order to ensure that the failures of the past do not become the failures of the future."

Jeff Skoll – Founder, The Skoll Foundation

Nonprofit Realities

Works Cited

Applegate, B. (2008). Challenges and Opportunities in Nonprofit Capacity Building. Nonprofit World. May/June 2008

Avolio, B., Yammarino, F. (2007). Transformational and Charismatic Leadership

Baker, M. (1998). Out with Confucius in Korea's big firms. (cover story). Christian Science Monitor, p. 1.

Burns, J. M. (1978). The crisis of leadership. In J. T. Wren (1995), The leader's companion: Insights on leadership through the ages (pp. 8-10). New York: The Free Press.

Cheney, T. (2006). A Decision Making Model to Enhance Corporate Ethics / Business Ethics / Social Responsibility. Business Renaissance Quarterly, 1(3), 15-20.

Clawson, J. G. (2006). Level three leadership: Getting below the surface (3rd ed.). Upper Saddle River: Pearson.

Covey, S. R. (2004). The 7 habits of highly effective people. Free Press.

Drumwright, M., & Murphy, P. (2004). How Advertising Practitioners View Ethics. Journal of Advertising, 33(2), 7-24.

Fisher, R.L. & Beimers, D. (2009). "Put me in, Coach" A Pilot Evaluation of Executive Coaching in the Nonprofit Sector. Nonprofit Management & Leadership. Vol. 19.

Goodboy, A.K. & McCroskey, J.C. (2008). Toward a Theoretical Model of the Role of Organizational Orientations and Machiavellianism on Nonverbal Immediacy Behavior and Job Satisfaction. Human Communication. Vol. 11.

Guttman, H. M. (2008). Leading high-performance teams. CEO Magazine, January/February, 33-35.

Harcourt, M., Lam, H., & Harcourt, S. (2005). Discriminatory practices in hiring: institutional and rational economic perspectives. International Journal of Human Resource Management, 16(11), 2113-2132. doi:10.1080/09585190500315125.

Herman, R.D. & Renz, D.O. (2008). Advancing Nonprofit Organizational Effectiveness Research and Theory. Nine Theses. Nonprofit Management & Leadership. Vol. 18.

Hersey, P. & Blanchard, K. H. (1995). Situational leadership. In J. T. Wren, The leader's companion: Insights on leadership through the ages (pp. 207-211). New York: The Free Press.

Jones, G.R. (2007). Organizational Theory, Design and Change. 5-th Ed. Upper Saddle River, NJ: Prentice Hall

Jones, J., & Middleton, K. (2007). Ethical Decision-Making by Consumers: The Roles of Product Harm and Consumer Vulnerability. Journal of Business Ethics, 70(3), 247-264. doi:10.1007/s10551-006-9109-2.

Judge, T. A., & Bono, J. E. (2000). Five-factor model of personality and transformational leadership. Journal of Applied Psychology, 85(5), 754-765.

Kaptein, M. (2009). Ethics Programs and Ethical Culture: A Next Step in Unraveling Their Multi-Faceted Relationship. Journal of Business Ethics, 89(2), 261-281. doi:10.1007/s10551-008-9998-3.

Kearney, E. & Gebert, D. (2009). Managing diversity and enhancing team outcomes: The promise of transformational leadership. Journal of Applied Psychology, 94(1), 77–89.

Leininger, C. (1997). The alignment of global management strategies, international communication approaches, and individual rhetorical choices. Journal of Business and Technical Communication, 11(3), 261-280.

Leslie, M. (2007). CULTURAL UNDERSTANDING. Infantry, 96(4), 7.

Manz, C. C. & Sims, H. P., Jr. (1991). SuperLeadership: Beyond the myth of heroic leadership. In Wren, J. T. (1995). The leader's companion: Insights on leadership through the ages (pp. 212-221). New York: The Free Press.

Manz, C. C. & Sims, H. P., Jr. (2001). The new superleadership. San Francisco, CA: Koehler Publishers, Inc.

Martin, K., & Johnson, J. (2008). A Framework for Ethical Conformity in Marketing. Journal of Business Ethics, 80(1), 103-109. doi:10.1007/s10551-007-9444-y

Sampson, S.D. & Moore, L.L. (2008). Is There a
Glass Ceiling for Women in Development?
Nonprofit Management & Leadership. Vol.
18.
Scott, W., (2003). Organizations: Rational, natural
and open systems (5-th ed.). Upper Saddle
River, NJ: Prentice Hall
Tierney, T.J. (2005). Understanding the Nonprofit
Sector's Leadership Deficit. The Leader of the
Future.
Trompenaars, F. & Hampden-Turner, C. (2002). 21
Leaders for the 21-st Century. McGraw-Hill.
Turner, C., Monk-Turner, E. (2007). Gender
differences in occupational status in the
South Korean labor market: 1988-1998.
International Journal of Social Economics,
34(8), 554.
Valentine, S. (2009). Ethics Training, Ethical
Context, And Sales And Marketing
Professionals' Satisfaction With Supervisors
And Coworkers. Journal of Personal Selling &
Sales Management, 29(3), 227-242.
Valentinov V. (2008). The Economics of Nonprofit
Organizations: In Search of an Integrative
Theory. Journal of Economic Issues.
Valentinov V. (2008). Toward an Incentive
Alignment Theory of Nonprofit Organization.
Journal of Economic Issues.
Weismann, M. (2009). The Foreign Corrupt
Practices Act: The Failure of the Self-
Regulatory Model of Corporate Governance in
the Global Business Environment. Journal of

Business Ethics, 88(4), 615-661. doi:10.1007/s10551-008-9966-y.

Wirtenberg, J. et al (2007). The Future of Organization Development in the Nonprofit Sector. Organization Development Journal. Vol.25.

Wren, T. J. (1995). The Leader's Companion. The Free Press New York.

Yang-Im L., Trim, P. (2008). The link between cultural value systems and strategic marketing; Unlocking the mindset of Japanese and South Korean managers. Cross Cultural Management, 15(1), 62.

Yukl, G. (2006). Leadership in organizations (6th ed.). Upper Saddle River, NJ: Pearson.

Zhang, H., 2003-05-27 "Studying Organizational Culture In Foreign Subsidiaries of Multinational Companies" Paper presented at the annual meeting of the International Communication Association, Marriott Hotel, San Diego, CA Online.

END

OTHER RESOURCES:

Visit www.ANG-MCC.com for more details!

Books by same author:

(Available at Amazon.com)

Trainings and Seminars: